GETTING IT RIGHT

Wedding Etiquette
by
Pat & Bill Derraugh

foulsham
London · New York · Toronto · Sydney

foulsham
Yeovil Road, Slough, Berkshire, SL1 4JH

Disclaimer:
While every effort has been made to ensure
the accuracy of all the information contained
within this book, neither the authors nor the
publisher can be liable for any errors.
In particular, since laws change from time to
time, it is vital that each individual should
check relevant legal details for himself or herself.

ISBN 0-572-01930-0

Printed in: Great Britain at
Cox & Wyman Ltd, Reading

Wedding Etiquette

The Wedding Colection:

CONTENTS

INTRODUCTION

There are many ways of getting married and of celebrating the occasion. From the traditional 'white wedding' followed by a grand reception and attended by all known friends and relatives, to the register office ceremony with just a selected few present.

Times and fashions change and 'courtship' as it was commonly called has taken on a different form, but despite the modern approach to many traditional customs the wedding still retains a great deal of its former sense of occasion. Many brides naturally cherish dreams of an idyllic wedding day; dreams which could sway them towards a church wedding rather than that of a register office.

To the bride and groom falls the overall organisation of the occasion but other parties involved, such as the best man, bride's mother and father and bridesmaids will need to be aware of their duties and will find this book useful.

With the changing fashions of our modern world it could sometimes be the girl who proposes marriage (without even waiting for a leap year), but whoever does the asking, if the answer is yes, then it's just the beginning of what could be a wonderful life together, and to start the adventure off smoothly you will find this book invaluable in the way that it can help you to organise the wedding day.

There are so many details to remember in the planning process that it is a good idea to have some *aide memoire* to ensure that nothing is overlooked. We have therefore included checklists at the end of the relevant chapters in the book which can be used to tick off each completed job. There are different lists for the principal participants and events, and any items on the lists which are not relevant can easily be deleted.

Here's hoping that your wedding day goes as planned and that the book helps to make the big day memorable.

1

GETTING ENGAGED

In 'the good old days' when grandmother was a young girl, there were strict conventions to be observed on the subject of marriage. It is more than likely that any young man she was 'walking out' with may even have been selected by her father through an arrangement with one of his friends or colleagues who had a son who could be considered acceptable as far as family, prospects and finances were concerned.

If the young man was suitably smitten by his beloved, then after a decent interval he would approach her father and request that he be allowed to ask for his daughter's hand in marriage. Permission having been given he would make his formal proposal, probably going down on one knee and hopefully she would say yes.

Times have changed and young people nowadays have many more opportunities to meet one another both socially and at work. They enjoy far more freedom generally, and when it comes to choosing a marriage partner and 'popping the question' it is their own choice. The man might still propose on bended knee but the general approach to marriage is far less formal than it used to be. The couple may even have been living together for a while as man and wife.

Whatever the circumstances leading up to the engagement they shouldn't detract from the fact that the happy couple have decided that they want to make a permanent commitment to each other and naturally they now want everybody to know that they intend getting married.

Breaking the News

The first people to be told the news should be the bride's parents and then the groom's parents. It is unlikely that the bride's father will be asked for his consent, although the law requires that in England and Wales the consent of parents or guardians is obtained for marriage, if either party is under the age of 18. They must be over 16. In Scotland the requirement is that they may marry provided that they are both at least 16 years of age on the day of their marriage.

After both sets of parents have been told, then the announcement can be made in general, usually by word of mouth to close friends and relatives. This will need to be done fairly quickly, to beat the grapevine! In some circles a press announcement may be considered necessary although these are far less common than they used to be.

The Engagement Ring

Traditionally the man has given his future bride a ring for her to wear as a sign of their betrothal. A gold ring, with one or more diamond stones, is probably the most popular design, but it is naturally a matter of choice. The days when a man produced a ring and placed it on his future bride's finger directly she had accepted his proposal, are probably over. This may happen if he has a family ring which he wants her to have, but more often than not they will find it best to go out and choose the engagement ring together.

The cost of rings varies enormously and it will depend on personal circumstances and future plans as to how much should be spent on the ring. If the engagement is to be a short one the decision may be to limit the spending on a ring and thus be in a better financial position to meet the numerous costs that will be coming shortly.

The selection of styles and settings of rings is also large and it is as well to have some idea of what is available in your price range before setting foot in the shop, otherwise there is a risk of being tempted to exceed your budget.

Apart from the traditional diamond engagement ring there are many attractive alternatives and birthstones have become a popular choice. The various stones are said to symbolise particular qualities as shown in the list below.

January	Garnet for Constancy
February	Amethyst for Sincerity
March	Bloodstone for Courage
April	Diamond for Innocence
May	Emerald for Success
June	Pearl for Health

July	Ruby for Love
August	Sardonyx for Married Happiness
September	Sapphire for Wisdom
October	Opal for Hope
November	Topaz for Fidelity
December	Turquoise for Harmony

Many girls like to give a present in return to mark this very special occasion. Suggestions for such a gift include gold signet ring, gold chain, tie-clip or cuff-links.

The Engagement Party

If there is to be an engagement party it should be held fairly shortly after the announcement is made so that it will serve as a suitable opportunity for congratulation and good wishes to be heaped on the happy couple – together with a few presents, no doubt.

The engagement party guest list may often be composed almost entirely of relations and can serve as an ideal opportunity for the prospective bride and groom to meet their future in-laws.

The home of the bride's parents is often the venue for the engagement party and traditionally the bride's father will bear the cost, although nowadays it is more likely that the cost will be shared, perhaps by the groom's father, who might also offer to hold the party at his home. Alternatively, it may be decided to hold the party in a hall with a more extensive guest list or to celebrate the occasion with a small dinner-party in a restaurant with just the immediate family and friends.

Wherever it is held it should be an informal affair with just two speeches: the bride's father announcing the engagement; and the bridegroom-to-be on behalf of his bride and himself, proposing the health of their parents.

The party is an ideal opportunity for the two sets of parents to meet if they haven't done so already, but if they live too great a distance apart for one set of parents to attend the party, then the newly engaged pair should make a visit to them as soon as possible so that at least the parents will see the happy couple and celebrate with them in some small way.

Breaking it Off

If, for some reason, there is subsequently a decision not to proceed with the wedding, gifts received from relatives or friends as a result of the engagement should be returned. If the two parties are still friends, they may decide to keep any presents given to each other during their time together, although it is usual for the girl to offer to return the ring, especially if she is the one to break off the engagement. It is the man's decision whether to accept it or not; if it is a family heirloom or his mother's engagement ring then he most probably will do so.

An engagement to marry is no longer a binding contract in the eyes of the law and nowadays we have a more philosophical approach to a break-up at this stage; far better to find out now, we say, than to discover his/her shortcomings after the wedding.

CHECKLIST 1.1 : THE ENGAGEMENT

Announce decision to her parents ☐

Announce decision to his parents ☐

Arrange for parents to meet ☐

Buy the ring ☐

   Traditional ring ☐

   Family ring or heirloom ☐

   Antique ring ☐

   Birthstone ☐

Present from her to him ☐
Although not necessary, a ring, cuff-links
or similar gift, preferably of gold or silver,
is acceptable

Tell relatives ☐

Tell close friends ☐

Engagement party/celebration ☐

Press announcement ☐

2

WHAT THE LAW SAYS ABOUT MARRIAGE

There are many ways, civil and religious, of taking the all-important step of getting married. This chapter deals with them mainly from the legal aspect.

ENGLAND AND WALES

In England and Wales a marriage can take place by means of (a) a ceremony performed in accordance with the rites of the Church of England, (b) a civil ceremony, or (c) a ceremony performed in accordance with the rites of a religious denomination other than the church of England.

Church of England

A marriage in accordance with the rites of the Church of England may be contracted in one of four ways:

1. By publication of banns.
2. By common licence (ordinary licence).

3. By special licence.
4. On the authority of a licence issued by a Super-intendent Registrar.

Generally, only one party to the marriage will be required to be a member of the Church of England and at least one of them should live in the parish of the church where the marriage is to take place (although certain exceptions as to residence may be made – for example in the case of marriage by special licence or sometimes if a person is an established member of a church outside his or her home parish and has his or her name entered on the electoral roll of that parish).

Although divorced persons may re-marry under civil law in a register office, the Church does not allow the re-marriage of divorced persons in church. Nevertheless, some ministers will agree to conduct a church wedding given these circumstances, but the normal procedure, if the couple really want the blessing of the Church, would be to have a civil wedding, with just a few close friends and relatives in attendance, followed by a Service of Blessing in church, possibly attended by many more family and friends. In this way the dress, ceremony and sense of occasion are maintained.

1. Publication of Banns: This is the method traditionally preferred by most people. The first thing to do is to call upon the minister of the church in which the marriage is to be solemnised and to ask him to allow the ceremony to take place in his church. If you would like another minister to officiate at the wedding (an old friend of the family, for example) that should also be discussed. When all the preliminaries have been satisfactorily completed, the minister will proceed to publish the banns.

The banns are published by being read aloud in church on three successive Sundays preceding the ceremony. They are usually read at the main service of the church. It is usual for the couple to be in church on at least one of the three occasions when the banns are read.

When the couple do not live in the same parish, the banns must be read in duplicate (a) in the parish of the man and (b) in the parish of the woman. A certificate should be obtained from the minister whose church is not being used to give to the minister in whose church the ceremony is to take place. This certificate states that the banns have been legally called, and without it the officiating minister cannot proceed with the wedding service.

Once the banns have been published, the wedding may be solemnised on any day within the three following months. It is best not to leave it too late. Marriages sometimes have to be delayed, and if there is insufficient time to arrange an alternative date within the three months the banns will have to be called again.

Since the system of marriage by banns has been devised to give publicity to the forthcoming wedding, it is fraudulent to substitute misleading names for the proper ones. When a person is generally known by a name which is not the one shown on his or her birth certificate, the banns should give the name more generally known, or should include both.

2. *Common Licence (Ordinary Licence):* The advantages of being married by common licence are that banns are unnecessary and only one clear day's notice is needed before the licence to marry is issued. It is therefore a much quicker procedure, and especially useful when for some reason the banns have not been properly published.

Common licences may be obtained from one of the Surrogates for granting licences in the diocese the minister at the church where the wedding is to take place may hold this title; if he does not, he will be able to tell you where you can obtain the licence. In applying at any of the above offices, it is necessary that one of the parties to the marriage should appear in person. The person making the application is required to sign a declaration stating that there is no legal reason why the marriage cannot properly take place and that either the man or the woman, or both, have lived for at least fifteen days prior to the application within the area served by the church that is to be used for the ceremony.

3. *Special Licence:* Special licences are issued only on the authority of the Archbishop of Canterbury from The Registrar of the Court of Faculties, 1 The Sanctuary, Westminster, London SW1P 3JT, and in cases when there is some special and urgent reason why the more ordinary methods of solemnising the marriage are unsuitable. When granted, a special licence permits the wedding to take place at any

time (within three months of the date of issue) and in any place, without restriction as to the residence of either party.

4. *Superintendent Registrar's Certificate:* A certificate to marry in accordance with the rites of the Church of England may also be given by a Superintendent Registrar.

The church where the marriage is to take place must be situated within the registration district of the Superintendent Registrar and either the man or the woman must have lived in the parish for seven days prior to giving notice.

The certificate will not be issued until twenty-one days after the notice is entered in the notice book and the ceremony may then take place within three months *from the day on which the notice was entered.* The marriage may be solemnised only by a minister of the Church of England and with the consent of the minister whose church is being used for the ceremony.

This method of authorisation is, however, very rarely used.

Register Office

When, for whatever reason, the couple do not wish to marry in a church, the ceremony can take place under civil law in a register office. In England and Wales notice should be given to the local Superintendent Registrar (whose address can be found under 'Registration of Births, Deaths and Marriages' in the telephone directory) who will arrange the marriage in one of three ways:

1. By Superintendent Registrar's Certificate.
2. By Superintendent Registrar's Certificate and Licence.
3. By Registrar General's licence.

With the exception of a licence issued by the Registrar General, notice may also be personally 'attested' before any local registrar of births and deaths or local registrar of marriages, but the notice is not held to have been duly given until it is received by the Superintendent Registrar and entered in his book.

1. Superintendent Registrar's Certificate: The official in this case will complete a form giving the names of the parties wishing to be married, their residences and their ages. The form also requires mention of the building in which the marriage is to take place and concludes with a declaration, to be signed, which states that there is no legal objection to the marriage.

Both the man and the woman must have lived in the area controlled by the registrar for seven days prior to giving notice, in which case only one of them need appear to make the declaration; or, if they live in different registration districts, they must each make the declaration before their own registrar and they must each have lived in their respective areas for seven days prior to the visit.

On being satisfied with the information supplied to him, the Superintendent Registrar will make the necessary entry in his notice book and, twenty-one days later, he will issue the certificate for the marriage. The ceremony can then take place at any time within the three months *following the entry in the notice book.*

2. *Superintendent Registrar's Certificate and Licence:* For marriage by certificate and licence, a similar declaration must be made and signed as for a marriage by certificate, but the residential qualifications are different. Only one of the couple need give notice, even though they may live in different registration areas, provided that one of them has lived in the area for fifteen days prior to the visit. However, the person not appearing must be within the borders of England and Wales or have his or her usual place of residence in England or Wales at the time notice is given.

One clear day after entering the notice, the Superintendent Registrar will issue the licence for the marriage (Sunday, Christmas Day and Good Friday are not counted). The licence is valid for three months following the date of entry in the notice book.

3. *Registrar General's Licence:* This method was introduced in 1970 and is reserved for cases of extreme illness where it would be impossible for the marriage to take place in a register office or other registered building. The licence permits the marriage to be solemnised in any place and at any time within three months from the date of entry in the notice book. There is no residence qualification and no statutory waiting period before the licence is

issued. Notice of marriage must be given (in person) by one of the couple to the local Superintendent Registrar.

Keeping on the Right Side of the Law

In addition to the formal procedures which have to be observed before any marriage can take place, there are a number of essential regulations concerning the conduct of the wedding ceremony itself and the freedom (in law) of the parties to marry.

(a) With the exception of the Jewish and Quaker ceremonies, the special licence and a licence issued by the Registrar General, no wedding can take place before 8.00 am or after 6.00 pm.

(b) A wedding cannot be private – hence the doors are not to be locked while the ceremony is proceeding.

(c) Before the ceremony, all relevant certificates or licences must be produced and handed to the registering official.

(d) Two persons must be present at the wedding, who will be required to sign their names as witnesses to the ceremony. They can be total strangers to each other and to the couple about to be married.

(e) People under 16 years of age may not marry. In the case of a person over 16 but under 18, written consent to marry must be given by the parents or other lawful guardians or guardian.

    If there is no parent or guardian to provide the necessary consent, application should be made to the courts for permission to marry. Also, if it is felt that a parent or guardian's permission has been unreasonably refused, an application to overrule their decision can be made to the courts.

(f) The marriage will not be valid if either party is already married.

(g) Neither party to a divorce may re-marry until the 'decree absolute' has been granted.

(h) The parties must be respectively male and female by birth.

(i) Both parties must be acting by consent and be of sufficiently sound mind to understand the nature of a marriage contract.

(j) Marriages are forbidden between people who are closely related. Those relationships prohibited *by law* are listed below. Additional restrictions may apply when a marriage is to be performed according to the rites of some religious denominations.

Prohibited Degrees of Relationship

A man may not marry his
mother
daughter
father's mother
mother's mother
son's daughter
daughter's daughter
sister
father's daughter
mother's daughter

Wedding Etiquette

wife's daughter
father's wife
son's wife
father's father's wife
mother's father's wife
wife's father's mother
wife's mother's mother
wife's son's daughter
wife's daughter's daughter
son's son's wife
daughter's son's wife
father's sister
mother's sister
brother's daughter
sister's daughter

A woman may not marry her
father
son
father's father
mother's father
son's son
daughter's son
brother
father's son
mother's son
husband's father
husband's son
mother's husband
daughter's husband
father's mother's husband
mother's mother's husband
husband's father's father

husband's mother's father
husband's son's son
husband's daughter's son
son's daughter's husband
daughter's daughter's husband
father's brother
mother's brother
brother's son
sister's son

The Marriage (Prohibited Degrees of Relationship) Act 1986 (for England, Scotland and Wales, but not Northern Ireland) allows a man to marry his mother-in-law, step-mother, step-daughter, or daughter-in-law without having to obtain a private Act of Parliament. By the same Act a woman may marry her father-in-law, step-father, step-son or son-in-law. However, for marriages between in-laws, the former spouses must have died. Marriages under this Act are not permitted with the calling of banns, but can take place in church by licence or by a Superintendent Registrar's certificate.

Any further information or clarification on whom you may or may not marry can be obtained from your local Superintendent Registrar.

FREE CHURCHES

The Order of Service used by the Free Churches (United Reformed, Baptist, Methodist and other Protestant bodies) is broadly similar to that of the Church of England. First of all, the chapel or building where the marriage is to take place must be registered for marriages and the registrar or other authorised person, (usually the minister) must be present to register the marriage. In addition to the 'authorised person' the marriage must be witnessed by at least two people who have reached the age of 18.

Although there is considerable similarity to the Church of England, each of the denominations has its own Order of Marriage which should be read beforehand. Your local church or one of the following organisations should be able to provide further help and advice.

Baptist Union of Great Britain and Ireland,
PO Box 44,
129 Broadway,
Didcot,
Oxfordshire OX11 8RT   Tel: 0235 512077

Methodist Church Press Service,
1 Central Buildings,
Westminster,
London   SW1H 9NH   Tel: 071 222 8010

United Reformed Church,
86 Tavistock Place,
London WC1H 9RT   Tel: 071 916 2020

OTHER DENOMINATIONS

If the marriage is to be conducted according to the rites of a religious denomination other than the Church of England, notice of marriage must still be given to the authorised registrar for the area concerned, who will grant a licence.

The building where the marriage is to take place must normally be registered for marriages, except in the case of Jewish weddings (see below) and the registrar or other authorised person must be present to register the marriage.

Roman Catholic Ceremony

A Roman Catholic priest will require up to six month's notice of an intended wedding and longer if possible. This is regarded as an essential period of time for preparation, whether both parties are Catholic or not. If one party is a non-Catholic, there will be a different form of service.

Banns are required to be read out in the parish churches of both bride and groom, except when one of them is a non-Catholic in which case no banns are read.

Jewish Ceremony

Civil law allows the Jewish wedding to take place anywhere; in a synagogue, private house, hired hall or in the open air. They can also take place at any time except the Jewish Sabbath or festival or fast days.

Quaker Ceremony

If only one partner is a member of the Society of Friends the other will be asked to state that he/she is in sympathy with the nature of the marriage and also to provide two letters of recommendation from members of the Society. Their Registering Officer gives advice and information then completes the required formalities for the wedding to proceed.

* * *

Your local religious body or one of the following organisations should be able to provide further help and advice:

Catholic Marriage Advisory Council,
23 Kensington Square,
London W8 5HN   Tel: 071 937 3781

Jewish Marriage Council,
23 Ravenhurst Avenue,
London NW4 4EL   Tel: 081 203 6311

Religious Society of Friends (Quakers),
Friends House,
173 Euston Road,
London NW1 2BJ   Tel: 071 387 3601

THE ROYAL NAVY

If one of the parties to the marriage is a serving member of the Royal Navy, the banns may be published aboard ship by the chaplain or commanding officer. In the case of a wedding in a register office or other registered building the commanding officer may record the particulars in place of the registrar and issue the necessary certificate twenty-one days after notice has been given.

SCOTLAND

The law on marriage in Scotland is now governed by The Marriage (Scotland) Act 1977. The couple can be married by a registrar, or assistant registrar, and the wedding will normally be held in his office. Alternatively, if they want a religious ceremony, they can be married by any clergyman, parson, priest or officer of any denomination who is entitled to undertake marriages under the Marriage (Scotland) Act. Whatever the type of wedding there must be two witnesses present who are at least 16 years of age.

In order to set the wedding wheels in motion, the couple must each get a marriage notice form from a registrar of births, marriages and deaths in Scotland. It does not matter which registrar is initially approached, but when the forms are filled in, they must be returned to the registrar for the district where the ceremony is to take place. Ideally, this should be done a month or more before the wedding date, and except in very exceptional circumstances a minimum of fifteen days notice must be given. If either party has been married before, the notice period is six weeks.

The marriage notice form is designed to establish whether the two parties are eligible to get married – for example in terms of age, existing marital status and sex – and that they are not related to each other in any way which forbids marriage. They have to sign a declaration that the information given is true; if it is not, the marriage will not be valid.

When the marriage notice forms are returned,

the registrar will also wish to see the relevant birth certificates. If either party has been married before, he or she will also need to produce a death certificate for the former spouse, or a copy of the divorce decree, remembering that a decree nisi from a court outside Scotland is not sufficient. If either party is domiciled outside the United Kingdom, evidence is required to show that there is no legal reason in their own country why the marriage should not proceed. When producing any foreign documents, it is important to get a certified translation, and if there is any doubt about what is needed, the registrar should be consulted.

If there is delay in getting any of the required documents, it is best to return the marriage notice form anyway, explain the situation, and get the documents to the registrar as soon as possible.

The registrar will check the facts given on the marriage notice form and then prepare a marriage schedule. For a civil marriage he will keep the schedule in his office until the wedding; but for a religious ceremony, it must be collected in person, not more than a week before the wedding. After the ceremony both parties sign the schedule, as do the two witnesses and whoever conducted the wedding. The schedule must be returned to the registrar within three days so that he can register the marriage.

As well as getting the marriage notice organised in good time, it is important to inform the person who will perform the ceremony of the preferred date . Particularly in towns, and at popular times of year, there is a need to book early.

If one party lives in England or Wales but is marrying someone who lives in Scotland (or whose parents live in Scotland) and wants the wedding to be in Scotland, it is possible to give notice without actually going north of the border to do so. Notice must be given to the Superintendent Registrar of the district in England or Wales, and similar notice given in Scotland in the normal way. Notices issued in England and Wales are valid in Scotland and vice-versa, provided only one of the parties is resident in Scotland. However, marriage by licence in a register office in England or Wales is not possible in this case.

NORTHERN IRELAND

Church of Ireland

Marriage in a church of the Church of Ireland may take place by means of:

1. Banns.
2. Licence.
3. Special Licence.
4. Certificate issued by a Registrar.

1. Banns: The banns may be read in the church where the ceremony is to take place if both partners are Protestant Episcopalians.

2. Licence: One or both partners must be Protestant Episcopalians and one must have spent fourteen days immediately prior to the service in the district of the church where it is to take place.

A Church of Ireland Licenser will issue the necessary licence after having received confirmation of the required seven days residence in the district prior to service of notice of the proposed marriage. Copies of said notice will be sent to the places of worship which the parties attend and seven days after service of notice on him, the Licenser may issue the licence.

The marriage must take place within three calendar months of the date of notice.

3. *Special Licence* - Provided one or both partners are Protestant Episcopalians a bishop may grant a special licence authorising the marriage to proceed at any time or place within his jurisdiction.

4. *Registrar's Certificate* - This authorises the marriage to take place in a church providing one or both of the partners are Protestant Episcopalians. If they live in different districts, separate applications must be made and the Registrar must send a copy of the notice of marriage to the clergymen of the places of worship attended by the partners and also to the clergyman of the church where the marriage is to be solemnised if this is different. At least one of the partners must have resided fifteen days in the district of the church where the marriage is to take place.

The Roman Catholic Church

Marriage in the Roman Catholic Church may take place by:
1. Episcopal Licence.
2. Banns.

3. Licence.
4. Certificate issued by a Superintendent Registrar of Marriage.

1. Episcopal Licence: and *2. Banns:* Both partners must be Roman Catholic and should apply to their parish priest or priests for information about the steps to be taken.

3. Licence: One or both partners must be Roman Catholic; where only one partner is Roman Catholic, notice in writing must be given to the person empowered to issue licences seven days before the licence shall be issued and that person must send copies of the notice to the clergymen of the places of worship which the partners attend.

4. Registrar's Certificate: This may be obtained to authorise marriage in a Roman Catholic Church when one of the partners is not Roman Catholic.

Presbyterian Church in Ireland

Marriage in the Presbyterian Church in Ireland can be authorised by means of:
1. Banns.
2. Licence.
3. Special Licence.

1. Banns: The banns may be read in the church or churches of which the parties are members and the wedding must take place in one of these churches. Authorisation of marriage by this method is not permissible if the wedding is going to take place in the church of any other denomination or if one of the marriage partners is a member of another church body, even if that is another Presbyterian church such as the Church of Scotland.

2. *Licence:* Marriage by licence requires that one or both of the parties must be members of the Presbyterian Church in Ireland. Consent from parents or guardians must be obtained if one or both of the partners is under 18 years of age (21 in the Republic of Ireland) and this proviso applies to any of the three forms of authorisation.

When application is made to the minister he will issue a certificate confirming that one of the partners has been a member of the congregation for at least the past month. The certificate should be produced to a Licensing Minister. Allowing at least seven days notice for granting of the licence, it will subsequently need to be produced to the officiating minister before the marriage ceremony takes place.

The time restrictions imposed in using this method of marriage are:
(a) residential qualification of 15 days within the Presbyterian area immediately prior to the wedding.
(b) the wedding must take place within three calendar months of the entry in the Licensing Minister's notice book.
(c) the wedding must take place within one calendar month of the date of the licence.

3. *Special Licence:* Once again the requirement is membership of the Presbyterian Church in Ireland

of one or both parties. The licence, which is issued by the Moderator of the General Assembly of the Presbyterian Church in Ireland, authorises the marriage to take place at any time or place in Ireland and is valid for three months. There is no residential requirement for either party.

* * *

Your local church or one of the following organisations should be able to provide further help and advice:

Catholic Marriage Advisory Council,
23 Kensington Square,
London W8 5HN　　　　Tel: 071 937 3781

Presbyterian Church in Ireland,
Church House,
Fisherwick Place 1,
Belfast BT1 6DW　　　　Tel: 0232 322284

The Registrar General,
General Register Office,
Oxford House,
49-55 Chichester Street,
Belfast BT1 4HF　　　　Tel: 0232 235211

MARRIAGES OF BRITONS ABROAD AND FOREIGN NATIONALS IN THE U.K.

If marriage abroad is contemplated, first find out what documents (if any) will be required for the marriage to be legal. You will probably be asked to provide a certificate of no impediment to marriage and also your birth certificate, proof of residency, proof of no convictions, etc. The extent of the requirements varies according to the regulations of each country. If you are still living in Britain, check with the foreign consul of the country concerned.

The marriage will generally be held to be legally valid under British law provided that it is performed in accordance with the law of the country in which it takes place and that none of the regulations in British law regarding the relationship of the parties or their freedom to marry are contravened. The marriage must also be monogamous. However, the situation varies according to individual circumstances and final judgement may rest on a court decision.

On the other hand, marriage under British law is not necessarily valid in every foreign country, so if a foreign national wishes to marry in the United Kingdom, he or she should consult their consul or other representative in Britain to ensure that the contemplated marriage ceremony will be accepted as legally binding in their own country. This applies whether the marriage is to a British subject or to someone of their own nationality.

THE CHURCH AND DIVORCE

In the *Church of England* a clergyman has the legal right to refuse to marry in church anyone whose previous partner is still alive. However, he will probably be prepared to conduct a Service of

Blessing at some time after the civil ceremony has been performed. Despite the Church's general ruling on this matter some ministers may still offer to perform the full wedding service.

The *Church of Scotland* will allow a church ceremony if either party has been married before, provided that the couple comply with the required notice period of six weeks. Banns will not be read in church as this requirement was abolished by the Marriage (Scotland) Act 1977.

Civil divorce is not recognised by the *Roman Catholic Church*. If re-marriage by such a person was contemplated it would have to be established that the first marriage was not recognised by the Roman Catholic Church. This would mean either that a declaration of nullity had been granted by a Roman Catholic Marriage Tribunal or that a previous marriage had not complied with Church Law.

Civil Re-marriage in England and Wales is allowed if the divorced person can produce a decree absolute. The re-marriage in a register office can then proceed in exactly the same way as a first marriage. The decree absolute is obtainable on application by the successful petitioner six weeks after the decree nisi which first pronounced the divorce.

Civil Re-marriage in Scotland is possible directly after the divorce is announced, because in Scotland there is no equivalent to the decree nisi; the decree is absolute immediately.

CHANGING YOUR NAME

A woman does not have to change her name when she gets married, although it is generally expected and usually makes life a little easier when making joint arrangements of a social or legal nature.

Sometimes a woman retains her maiden name for business purposes, when to change it would be inconvenient or potentially damaging. Having two separate identities is confusing, but it may be the best solution in the circumstances.

If you do decide to change your name, however, there are lots of people who will want to know about it. It may take a little time to get round all the relevant authorities and organisations, but here are some of the more important ones to note:

> Employer, bank, building society, savings accounts, insurance companies, credit card companies, passport office (you don't have to change the name on your passport, but it is usually more convenient if you do), Inland Revenue, Department of Health and Social Security, DVLC (for change of driver's licence and vehicle registration documents), your doctor and your dentist.

If you are going abroad on honeymoon, you will require a passport. The issue of family passports with particulars of husband and wife included has been discontinued. If you wish to travel abroad in your married name, leaflet PD1 and Form PD2 need to be obtained from the Post Office for the issue of a post-dated passport. New applicants will also require Form A, while those who wish to have existing passports amended, also need to complete Form C.

Completed application forms should be sent to the Passport Office for your particular area. These are listed on the application form and you should allow at least one month for the application to be processed and up to three months if applying between February and June.

CHECKLIST 2.1: CHURCH OF ENGLAND

Both parties must be over 16 ☐

If under 18, obtain parents' consent ☐

For divorced persons, obtain a decree
absolute and agreement of the minister ☐

Choose church ☐

Apply to minister of church ☐

Arrange for publication of banns ☐

Ask minister of church to publish banns ☐

If one partner living in different parish,
also arrange for banns to be called in that
parish ☐

If both partners living in different parishes,
also arrange for banns to be called in those
parishes ☐

Banns to be read out during morning service on:

1. .... ☐

2. .... ☐

3. .... ☐

Attend calling of banns ☐

OR Obtain a common licence ☐

If one partner living in parish for preceding
15 days, he/she can apply in person ☐

What the Law says about Marriage

Obtain licence ☐

OR Obtain a special licence ☐

Apply to the Archbishop of Canterbury ☐

Provide sworn statement of reasons special licence required ☐

Obtain licence ☐

OR Obtain Superintendent Registrar's Certificate ☐

If one partner living in district for preceding 7 days, he/she can apply in person ☐

Notice entered ☐

Obtain certificate (after 21 days) ☐

Finalise date of ceremony............................... ☐

Finalise place of ceremony .... ☐

CHECKLIST 2.2: THE REGISTER OFFICE

Both parties must be over 16

If under 18, obtain parents' consent

For divorced persons, obtain a decree absolute

Provide details of names, ages,addresses etc.

Provide statements that there are no
legal reasons why the marriage should
not take place, such as death certificate
of former spouse or decree absolute

Choose register office

Obtain Superintendent Registrar's Certificate

If both living in district for preceding
7 days, one partner can apply in person

If living in different districts for
preceding 7 days, each partner must
apply in person to respective
Superintendent Registrars

Notice entered in Superintendent
Registrar's notice book

Obtain certificate (after 21 days)

OR Obtain Superintendent Registrar's
Certificate and Licence

If one partner living in district for
preceding 15 days, he/she can apply
in person

What the Law says about Marriage

Other partner living in England or
Wales at time notice given ☐

Notice entered in Superintendent
Registrar's notice book ☐

Obtain certificate (after one clear day) ☐

OR Obtain Registrar General's Licence ☐

Apply in person to Superintendent
Registrar ☐

Obtain licence ☐

Finalise date of ceremony .... ☐

Finalise place of ceremony .... ☐

CHECKLIST 2.3: SCOTLAND

Both parties must be 16 or over

Obtain marriage notice forms

Return marriage notice forms with birth
certificates, and death certificate or divorce
decree certificate if second marriage

Collect marriage schedule

Finalise date of ceremony ....

Finalise place of ceremony ....

Sign marriage schedule and arrange
for it to be signed by two witnesses and
person who conducted the wedding

Return marriage schedule to registrar
within three days

3

THE WEDDING PREPARATIONS

The announcement of your engagement is the first step in the process of getting married and marks the beginning of much careful planning and preparation for the wedding day itself.

THE TIME AND PLACE

Once you have decided on the form of ceremony you would like and approximately when it is to take place, you should go to see the minister or registrar concerned so that the proper religious and/or legal arrangements can be made.

At the same time it is wise to ensure that a suitable venue for the reception will be available on the chosen day; in fact it is often necessary to book the reception before the church. After all, the church can accommodate a number of weddings on one day, but the hall or hotel is probably available for just one.

If you are going to be married in church you should discuss with the minister the details of the ceremony including the style and order of service, whether or not a choir should be present, the music that is to be played and the possibility of bell-ringing. Also find out about the fees (there are basic legal statutory fees, but other church costs are at the discretion of the minister), and ask if your guests will be allowed to take photos in the church or throw confetti in the church grounds. The minister will want to talk to you about the significance of a church wedding and he may invite you to attend a marriage preparation course which takes a broad look at all the issues involved.

In all aspects of the marriage ceremony the minister really is the expert and his advice and guidance will be well worth having.

Equally, if you have decided on a civil ceremony, you should go to see the local Superintendent Registrar as soon as possible. Apart from the legal formalities, you should find out how many guests can be accommodated at the ceremony and whether photographs may be taken in the register office.

Most people deciding to get married in this way do so either because they want a quiet ceremony with no fuss or because a marriage in church would conflict with their own beliefs.

INVITATIONS

The invitations should be sent out well in advance of the date set for the wedding – six to eight weeks is about right.

The list of guests is usually drawn up by the bride and her mother in consultation with the bridegroom and his parents. The engagement list will serve as a useful guide, although there are sure to be some omissions and additions.

The invitations themselves are normally composed in the third person and sent from the bride's parents. The most popular wording is:

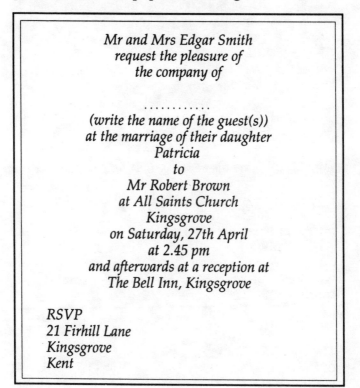

Mr and Mrs Edgar Smith
request the pleasure of
the company of

. . . .
(write the name of the guest(s))
at the marriage of their daughter
Patricia
to
Mr Robert Brown
at All Saints Church
Kingsgrove
on Saturday, 27th April
at 2.45 pm
and afterwards at a reception at
The Bell Inn, Kingsgrove

RSVP
21 Firhill Lane
Kingsgrove
Kent

For those guests who are being invited to the reception only, you will need evening cards with wording such as:

Mr and Mrs Edgar Smith
request the pleasure of
the company of

. . . .

at the Evening Reception
to be held at
The Bell Inn, Kingsgrove
on Saturday, 27th April
at 7.00 pm
to celebrate the marriage of their daughter
Patricia
to Robert Brown

RSVP
21 Firhill Lane
Kingsgrove
Kent

If the number of guests is quite low, the invitations may be written by hand on suitably attractive stationery. More often, however, they are printed. Visit a stationer's and have a look at the range of cards and styles of lettering that are available. Black is the traditional colour for the lettering. If you want to order reply cards, order of service sheets or cake boxes, you can see to this at the same time.

The Wedding Preparations

If the occasion is a second wedding for one or both of the partners – especially after divorce – it is likely to be a much less formal affair. The bride and groom will probably host the affair and send out invitations with less formal wording such as:

Patricia Smith and Robert Brown invite you to their wedding at All Saints Church, Kingsgrove, on Saturday, 27th April at 2.45 pm (and afterwards to a reception at The Bell Inn, Kingsgrove).

In the unfortunate event of a family bereavement or severe illness you will probably want to postpone the wedding, and notices will have to be sent to all those invited to attend. A plain statement of the facts is quite sufficient, with notice of the new date for the wedding, if one has been arranged.

Owing to the recent death (illness) of Mr Edgar Smith, the wedding between Patricia Smith and Mr Robert Brown at All Saints Church, Kingsgrove at 2.45 pm on Saturday, 27th April, has been postponed (to 4.00 pm on Friday, 30th May).

Formal replies to invitations should be sent promptly (within three days of receiving the invitation) and are also traditionally drawn up in the third person. The following is the usual wording:

Mr and Mrs John Clemence thank Mr and Mrs Edgar Smith for their kind invitation to their daughter's wedding and to the reception and will be most happy to attend.

However, when the guests are very close friends of the host and hostess a brief, informal thank-you note will do just as well.

WEDDING PRESENTS

The business of giving or receiving wedding presents is always a little daunting – to both sides. Visions of dozens of toasters and electric kettles loom before the eyes of the engaged couple, while the guests are naturally concerned that their carefully chosen gifts should be received with the proper appreciation.

Even the best laid plans go wrong sometimes – but there are some practical steps you can take to ensure that this particular wedding custom turns out happily (as far as possible) for all concerned.

There are really only two rules to remember:

1. Have a wedding present list prepared for anyone who wishes to consult it.
2. Be sure to write thank-you letters to everyone who sends you a present.

1. The Wedding List

Once you have compiled a list of the presents that you would like, you should make a number of copies and let people have one when they ask. Ask them, when they have bought their present, to return the list with the item they have bought crossed off. The list can then be handed to somebody else and although this method isn't guaranteed to avoid duplication it is probably bettered only by employing the services of a large store. By this method you compile your list from the items in that store, guests then ring the store, make their purchase and the store adjusts the list. This method has obvious drawbacks but may be worth considering.

The list itself should contain a good number of inexpensive as well as expensive presents, and should run to more items than you actually expect to receive. This avoids the possibility of the last guest to see the list being left to buy the colour television set!

Traditional wedding presents include items of china, glass, cutlery and kitchen utensils, garden tools, linens and other home accessories. More expensive gifts such as carpets and furniture are usually reserved for very close relatives or groups of friends banding together to share the costs.

There is however, no reason why you should think only in terms of fitting out the home. Books, pocket calculators, typewriters or sports equipment may be more useful to you and more urgently required. So do consider what your real needs are before finally drawing up the list.

2. Thank-you Letters

Although you can, if you like, ignore the need for a wedding list and perhaps even survive the resultant chaos, the same cannot be said of the need to write thank-you letters. It is so obviously discourteous and hurtful not to thank people who sent you presents that you should be especially careful not to leave anybody out. A methodical approach is the only answer.

Whenever you receive a present, make a note of what it is, who sent it and when it arrived. Write to the person concerned as soon as possible, thanking them for the gift and put a tick against their name when the letter is in the post.

This task traditionally falls to the bride, but if the bridegroom has received any personal gifts, he should reply to the senders on his own behalf.

Displaying the Presents

It is natural for the guests to want to see the wedding presents, and a display may be arranged at the reception or in the bride's parents' home. But there are certain risks involved. If the display is to be at an outside reception, perhaps at a big hotel, there may be a chance of some petty thieving from uninvited 'guests'. Moreover, you will be effectively advertising the contents of your future home to anyone who happens to be in the vicinity.

For that reason, it is usually safer to stage the display at a private house. The only snag is that some guests feel embarrassed to see their own relatively inexpensive presents ranged against other more valuable items. It will help if you dispense with the usual custom of using name tags to accompany the presents: if cheques have been received, you should set out cards stating simply 'cheque from ...' without divulging the amounts. The same applies to a display set up at the reception.

THE WEDDING RING

There is a superstition which claims that it is un-lucky to buy engagement and wedding rings on the same day. Even so, when buying the wedding ring it is a good idea to see if it looks 'suited' alongside the engagement ring.

Fashion may be followed when choosing the wedding ring, but often the simple style proves to be the best choice; never looking old-fashioned even after many years, simply traditional.

Most marriage services include the giving and receiving of a ring, although the Quakers are an exception, but it is still usual for the groom to give his bride a ring and this is often done directly after the ceremony when the register is signed.

DRESSING FOR THE OCCASION

The Bride's Dress

Choosing a wedding dress that will look and feel absolutely right on the day is one of the most important (and enjoyable) decisions the bride must make during the run-up to the ceremony.

The eventual choice will largely depend on the significance you attach to the dress itself and the sort of wedding you would like it to be. You may opt for the traditional white silk or lace dress with head-dress and veil, or choose a different colour such as cream or oyster, or a patterned dress.

If the wedding is to take place in a register office, you can still wear a traditional 'white wedding' dress, if that is what you would really like.

Whichever kind of dress you choose, give yourself plenty of time to look around and try on different examples. You should also allow time for the dress to be altered, if necessary, or made, if you are having one specially designed or made from a pattern.

Dresses for the Bridesmaids

The bride chooses the bridesmaids' dresses (and the pages' outfits), the main criteria being that they should complement her own wedding outfit. A dramatic contrast in colour, for example, will do little to enhance the bridal procession – or the wedding photographs. It might also look a little odd if the bride appeared in a plain dress while the bridesmaids were adorned with frills and lace. Bear in mind too, that bridesmaids vary in size, shape and colouring. You are trying to find something to suit them all, so avoid too much finery, or colours that are too strident.

Male Fashion

If the wedding is to be a very formal affair, the principal men will wear morning suits. This includes the bridegroom, the best man, the ushers and both fathers.

Generally, morning suits are either all grey, or consist of a black tailed coat and pin stripe trousers. They look good in the wedding photographs with accessories such as hats and gloves, although these can be rather a nuisance as more time will be spent carrying them and getting them mixed up than actually wearing them.

The morning suits may be hired or bought off the peg, or you could have one tailor made. For the majority however, hiring a suit will be the best answer. Remember that the summer months are the most popular for weddings and formal social functions and reserve your suit well in advance.

The favourite alternative for most weddings is a well-cut two or three-piece lounge suit – which will form a welcome addition to the wardrobe after the great event. The principal men should take their cue from the bridegroom when deciding on what to wear. They should not outshine him on the big day.

THE FLOWERS

Flowers are a very important part of every church wedding. Usually there will be bouquets or posies for the bride and bridesmaids and buttonholes for the principal men, and the church and reception area will be decorated with displays. There may also be sprays or corsages for the two mothers, and the bride may wish to wear a head-dress of fresh flowers or attach just one flower to her hair or veil.

The bouquets can be chosen from a selection of designs suggested by the florist – who will also be the best person to ask about suitable flowers for the church and reception.

If the arranging is not to be carried out professionally, the flowers may still need to be ordered several weeks in advance of the ceremony, especially if the preference is for unusual or out of season flowers. They should not be collected until one or two days before the wedding, when the larger displays are arranged. The bouquet, buttonholes and other dress flowers are usually delivered or collected on the morning of the wedding and the dress flowers are distributed at the church before the ceremony.

It will be necessary to get the permission of the minister to decorate the church, and arrange a time when this can be conveniently carried out. He may be able to suggest someone who can help, in return for a small donation.

It may also be possible to combine with other couples who are getting married in the church on the same day – the minister should be able to supply names and addresses.

When choosing the flowers, remember to take into account the character and size of the church and reception areas. A large, formal display, for example, would look out of place in a small room or a country church. It is also a good idea to have a theme – of colours and/or varieties – running through from the bride's bouquet to the flowers used in the church and reception. As with the wedding dresses, aim for a sympathetic blend of colour and form.

If the wedding is to take place in a register office, it may already be decorated with flowers. Check with the Superintendent Registrar. If not, you may be able to arrange for a simple display to be set up before the ceremony.

THE PHOTOGRAPHS

Your wedding day should be one of the most memorable days of your life, so it is imperative that you have a beautiful set of photographs to remind you of it.

A professional photographer should be your first choice and you may find that some acquaintance who has recently married can recommend one. Otherwise, try looking in the windows of local photographers and see if you can pinpoint anything in the display of their work that attracts you. Ask to see further examples of work and start comparing possible costs.

You will need to agree with the photographer beforehand any specific photographs that you would like to be taken before, during or after the ceremony. Check with the minister as to whether he imposes restrictions on photography inside the church.

Videos

If you are contemplating video coverage of your wedding, then you will have to make enquiries of a number of people who offer this service. It may be advantageous from a cost point of view to use the same firm to take both the still photographs and the video. Once again you will need the minister's approval, since the video team will need to visit the church to test not only for lighting, but also for angles and sound.

THE PRESS

Even if the engagement has not been announced in a newspaper, many couples like to insert a notice giving the time and place of the forthcoming wedding, to appear a few days before the chosen date. Newspapers usually have their own style for this, so check in the selected one for suitable wording.

The newspaper may also publish an account of the wedding, sometimes by sending a reporter/photographer, but more often by issuing a standard form to be filled in and returned after the wedding with a photograph.

CHECKLIST 3.1: SUGGESTED WEDDING LIST

Many of these ideas can be divided into several specific suggestions, for example, glasses can be divided into the various types you would like. You may wish to specify particular colours or styles you would prefer for many items. You will also need to consider the more personal gifts you would like to add.

Baking tins
Bathroom cabinet
Blankets
Bread bin
Bookcase
Bowl, bucket etc.
Carpets
Carpet sweeper
Casserole dishes
Clock
Corkscrew
Coffee grinder
Coffee maker
Coffee table
Cookery book
Cruet set
Cushions
Cutlery
Dinner service
Door mat
Duvet
Egg rack
Electric drill

Feather duster
Food processor
Fridge
Garden fork
Garden furniture
Garden spade
Glasses
Kitchen knives
Laundry basket
Lawn mower
Microwave oven
Mirror
Mincer
Mixer
Oven
Oven gloves
Pedal bin
Personal stationery
Pictures
Pillows
Place mats
Pyrex dishes
Rugs

Saucepans
Saw, hammer etc.
Scales
Sheets
Spice rack
Storage jars
Table and chairs
Table lamp
Tablecloth
Tea service
Tea towels
Telephone table
Three-piece suite
Trolley
Toaster
Tool box
Tools
Towels
Vacuum cleaner
Vases
Vegetable rack
Wall can opener
Washing machine
Wine rack

CHECKLIST 3.2: THE PHOTOGRAPHS/VIDEO

Select and book photographer ☐

Select and book video team (if different) ☐

Obtain minister's approval for in-church video ☐

Arrange programme of sequential items for video ☐

Photographs may be requested of:

Bride's dressing table ☐

Before leaving for the wedding ☐

Leaving the house ☐

The best man and groom before the ceremony ☐

Arriving at the church/register office ☐

Inside the church (with minister's permission) ☐

Signing the register (with minister's permission) ☐

Leaving the church/register office ☐

Bride and groom ☐

Couple with parents ☐

Couple with best man, bridesmaids and pages ☐

Couple with bride's family ☐

The Wedding Preparations

Couple with groom's family ☐

Couple with friends ☐

Bridesmaids and pages ☐

At the reception ☐

Cutting the cake ☐

Discuss any special effects required, e.g.
couple in wine glass ☐

Arrange for proof photographs to be made
available at the reception ☐

Take orders for photographs from
family and guests ☐

Give order to photographer ☐

Distribute photographs ☐

4

THE PRINCIPAL PLAYERS

In this chapter we look at the duties of the principal players in a traditional English wedding. We have based the timetable of events primarily on a Church of England wedding, but the duties involved still apply to a large extent on whether the wedding is in church, chapel or register office and for many other creeds, including Roman Catholic and some Free Churches, although it cannot be applied to foreign nationals marrying in this country or to weddings of members of the Jewish and Quaker faiths.

The Marriage Ceremony plays continuously around the country, throughout the year. Naturally it becomes more popular during the summer months, especially June, which is named after the goddess Juno, the adored and faithful wife of Jupiter, who is the protector of women and marriage, and Juno is said to bestow special blessings on those who wed in her month:

> Married in the month of roses – June
> Life will be one long honeymoon.

The crowds who attend these weddings, turning up on the wedding day in their best outfits and bearing gifts, have little occasion to think of the preparations that have been under way for many months and the principal players who will ensure that everything goes smoothly.

There are just half a dozen of these principal players, all playing their part, large or small, and invariably everybody goes away saying what a grand day it was, and didn't the bride look lovely.

The bride is of course the undoubted star. It is her day. She is going to be the centre of attention for the entire day, even the groom has a secondary role, and the other players form a supporting cast.

THE BRIDE

Every bride wants to look her best on her wedding day, when she will be the centre of attention for the bridegroom and all the guests, and the feature of wedding photographs and videos.

Invariably the bride's main concern will be her wedding dress. The long wedding gown is still very popular and many brides marrying in a register office choose the traditional wedding gown, although probably without a train or long veil. White is still the main choice of colour, even for some brides who are pregnant or when the bride and bridegroom have been living together as man and wife before the wedding.

Wedding dresses can be hired, ready made or professionally made for you by a dressmaker. Alternatively, a close friend or relation may offer you the use of her wedding dress. This may be a very good proposition if the style suits you and also if any necessary alterations are minimal.

Wedding Etiquette

Duties

The bride's main function on this, her special day, is to look beautiful. She will have the assistance of her mother and the chief bridesmaid when she is getting ready. Then, with her father or whoever is giving her away, she leaves for the church, making sure that she doesn't arrive early.

At the church entrance the chief bridesmaid will arrange the bride's dress, veil and train. The bride then takes her father's right arm and proceeds slowly down the aisle to where the bridegroom and best man are waiting. She then hands her bouquet to the chief bridesmaid in order to leave her hands free when the ring is put on. At the end of the marriage service, the bride accompanies the groom in the procession to the vestry to sign the register. The bride and groom then lead the procession out of church with the bride on the left arm of her husband.

After the photographs have been taken outside the church, the bride and groom are the first to leave for the reception where they will shortly be joined by the bride's parents and the groom's parents and together form a welcoming line for the arriving guests.

At the end of the meal come the toasts and speeches and though the bridegroom speaks on behalf of his bride and himself, the bride may wish to say a few words of her own.

At some time the bride throws her bouquet to the waiting bridesmaids, the tradition being that the one who catches it will be the next to marry. Sometimes of course the eager, outstretched hands belong to some of the young, unmarried guests! The moment for this ritual is either when the bride is going upstairs to change into her going-away outfit or when she is getting into the car, ready to depart in a shower of confetti.

Expenditure

Families nowadays are more likely to make alternative financial arrangements for some of the major expenses, so although traditionally the bride's father pays for her wedding dress, she may decide that she will pay for her own dress or alternatively the bridesmaid's dresses.

She may buy a ring for the groom and small presents for the bridesmaids which can be given to them either before the ceremony or at the reception.

THE BRIDEGROOM

As mentioned earlier, the bridegroom has only a supporting role on the day. If his earlier decision in the choice of best man was a good one, then he will have saved himself some anxious moments on the day, as a good best man can do a great deal to assist the groom throughout the day.

Duties

Before the wedding day the groom will decide, probably with the help of his bride-to-be, what the male order of dress will be. If his choice is morning suits, then the best man, ushers and fathers of the bride and groom will be required to follow suit.

As the wedding draws near many of the groom's male friends and colleagues will be keen to know when and where the stag party will be. It is advisable, for everybody's sake – and especially the groom's – to have that particular celebration at least two days before the wedding, so that any after-effects have time to be dispelled.

The groom will have the best man in attendance on the morning of the wedding, lending him moral support and making sure he gets to the church about twenty minutes before the ceremony is due to start. Before they set off for the church the groom can give the best man the wedding ring and also the wedding documents. He may also want the best man to look after other items such as tickets and passports and possibly car keys. If the bride and groom are changing into going-away clothes at the reception venue, the groom should have these ready to entrust to the best man.

Having arrived early at the church, the groom now has to endure a waiting and wondering period until the bride's arrival. After the service he accompanies the bride in the procession to the vestry to sign the register. The happy couple then lead the procession out of church with the bride on the left arm of her husband.

After the photographs have been taken outside the church, the bride and groom are the first to leave for the reception where they will shortly be joined by the bride's parents and the groom's parents and together form a welcoming line for the arriving guests. The recognised order is:

the bride's mother and father
the groom's mother and father
the bride and groom

The bridegroom will be called upon to reply to the toast made by the bride's father and will speak on behalf of his bride and himself. Some information on the subject of speeches will be found at the end of this chapter.

Expenditure

The bridegroom's expenditure starts with the engagement ring. He isn't expected to stand the cost of the stag party; everybody present pays a share. Naturally he will pay for his own outfit, whether bought or hired, and if hired he might pay for the best man's also. He may wish to buy the best man a small gift as a memento of the occasion.

The bridegroom also pays church or register office expenses and should hand the money to the best man on the wedding morning in order that he may pay the clergyman or verger.

Naturally the groom will pay for his bride's wedding ring and also her bouquet together with those of the bridesmaids; also buttonholes for himself and all the principal men, and sprays for the two mothers. He will also pay for the car to take him and the best man to the church and the car to transport himself and his bride to the reception.

Last, but by no means least, he will pay for the honeymoon.

THE BEST MAN

In the majority of cases the best man will be either a close friend or relative of the bridegroom. His main function is to look after the groom and to lend his assistance generally to see that the big day goes without a hitch. Together, the bridegroom and best man choose the ushers whose main role will be to show the wedding guests to their seats in the church, hand out service sheets or prayer books and help the best man in making sure that everybody has transport to the reception.

Duties

The best man's main task, of course, is to get the bridegroom to the church on time, but prior to the actual wedding day he has several important jobs which mustn't be neglected. Traditionally he has to make sure that everything is in order regarding the groom's clothes, both for the wedding and also his going-away clothes. These the best man may be entrusted with and have to take to the reception venue if the newlyweds are leaving for their honeymoon directly from there. He may also be asked to look after the bride's suitcase. If suits are being hired it is likely that the bridegroom and best man will go to the hire shop together and if the bridegroom is in a magnanimous mood he may foot the bill for the best man's outfit, but generally speaking the best man pays for his own suit.

His other major pre-wedding day job is to organise the stag party which, from the men's point of view of course, is a very important event. The best man should ensure that it is not held on the eve of the wedding, just in case there are any celebratory after-effects.

On the morning of the big day, if special order of service sheets have been printed, he has to collect them from the bride's mother and get them to the church, or perhaps delegate the job to an usher. Buttonholes for himself, the groom and the ushers could probably be collected at the same time together with any telemessages for the happy couple.

Having settled all the incidentals he sets off for the groom's house where he will take charge of any documents, such as tickets, passports, wedding documents and of course, the ring.

Having made sure that the groom is looking his best, the best man should get him to the church about twenty minutes before the service is due to start. During the service the best man's prime function is to produce the ring or rings at the appropriate moment. After the service he will accompany the chief bridesmaid in the procession to the vestry for the signing of the register and may be called upon to sign as a witness.

After the photographs are finished, transport to the reception has to be arranged by the best man, as mentioned earlier. Alternatively, he may entrust this task to the ushers and accompany the bridesmaids to the reception. If the bride and groom are leaving the reception by car, then the best man may have the additional task of parking the car nearby and looking after the keys.

At the reception, the best man makes a short

speech, reads out a selection of telemessages and tells the guests the rest of the programme for the reception. Some information on speeches will be found at the end of this chapter.

If the suits were hired for the wedding the best man will no doubt have to return the bridegroom's, together with his own.

Expenditure

Apart from buying himself a new suit or hiring an outfit, the best man's expenses are relatively light. The bridegroom will provide him with the money to pay any wedding fees and any other incidental expenses.

THE BRIDESMAIDS AND PAGES

The choice of bridesmaids and pages can sometimes pose problems for the bride, not only in the number of attendants, but their respective ages. Whatever the final choice, the selection of chief bridesmaid will no doubt be decided quite early on in the proceedings. She will probably be a sister or close friend of the bride. If she is already married herself, her title is matron of honour, but her duties remain the same.

Duties of Chief Bridesmaid (or Matron of Honour)

Her initial task might be to assist the bride in her choice of wedding dress and perhaps at the same time decide on the bridesmaid's dresses. Alternatively all the dresses can be hired for the day.

On the wedding day she will go to the bride's house in the morning and help her with her preparations: dressing, make-up, hair etc. She can also help any younger bridesmaids to dress and give them some last-minute instructions. The bridesmaids and pages then proceed to the church and wait at the entrance.

When the bride arrives at the church, the chief bridesmaid will arrange the bride's dress, veil and train, then follow her in procession down the aisle. She will probably then be handed the bride's bouquet for the duration of the ceremony.

After the service she will accompany the best man in the procession to the vestry for the signing of the register and may be called upon to sign as a witness. She can then return the bride's bouquet to her and then, once again accompanied by the best man, follow the bride and groom from the church.

At the reception she has no specific duties, though she might assist the bride in her going-away preparations.

Expenditure

Traditionally the bridesmaids and pages pay for their own outfits, although the bride might offer to pay under certain circumstances, particularly if the outfits are unlikely to be worn again.

THE USHERS

Duties

The ushers should arrive at the church early, three-quarters of an hour before the service is due to start. They are required to greet people at the church entrance, ascertain whether they are guests of the bride or groom, then show them to their seats, handing them order of service sheets or prayer books at the same time. Bride's guests are seated on the left of the aisle and the groom's on the right, although if there is an extreme imbalance it is permitted to discreetly even out the numbers.

After the ceremony the ushers should help the best man to ensure that everyone has transport to the reception.

THE BRIDE'S MOTHER

The bride's mother takes no official part in the ceremony yet to all intents and purposes she organises the wedding every step of the way.

Duties

The whole thing starts for her with the organisation of the guest list and sending out the invitations. Bearing in mind that her husband is footing the bill for many of the wedding day costs, she has to compile a guest list which is fairly balanced for both bride and groom. In actual fact there are often two lists: one for the wedding service followed by the reception and another list of guests invited to the reception only.

Booking the hall or hotel for the reception may be done by her or alternatively by the bride and groom. She will also order the wedding cake, or perhaps even make it herself, arrange for the printing of order of service sheets and order wedding cars for the bride and her father, the bridesmaids, and of course herself and any other guests who require transport from her house to the church. Then she must organise the flowers: buttonholes for the guests, bouquets and decorations for the church and reception. Although the bridegroom traditionally pays for the buttonholes and bouquets for the principal players, it is better if they are all ordered together in order to maintain a theme of colours or varieties. She will also need to book the photographer and make the catering arrangements for the reception if it is being held in a hall rather than a hotel.

These are just the major items; there are doubtless a thousand and one minor problems to solve and she must ensure that not too many of them cause last-minute panics which might upset the arrangements on her daughter's big day.

On the morning of the wedding, she will help her daughter get ready and attend to all the last – minute details as well as getting herself ready. If the reception is to be held at home she will have considerably more to do in preparing for the returning guests.

At the close of the service she joins the bridegroom's father as the wedding party proceeds to the vestry for the signing of the register. She comes out of the church, still with the bridegroom's father, then after the photographs outside the church she rejoins her husband and they should be the first, after the newlyweds, to depart to the reception where they will greet the guests as they arrive.

THE BRIDE'S FATHER

Traditionally the bride's father pays for almost everything on the occasion of his daughter's wedding, but very often nowadays the groom or the groom's father will offer to contribute some part of the cost. Although tradition also says that the bride's mother organises the wedding, no doubt she will be assisted in many ways by her husband, since there is a considerable amount of preparation involved and decisions to be made.

Duties

On the subject of dress the bride's father complies with the bridegroom. If the groom decides that the order of dress will be morning suits, then all the male attendants are required to dress in the same fashion and that includes the bride's father and the bridegroom's father.

The main duty of the bride's father is to give his daughter away on her wedding day. When she is ready to leave the house, he accompanies her to the church, then escorts her down the aisle. At the appropriate time in the service when the minister asks who is giving the bride away, he will take his daughter's right hand and place it in the hand of the minister.

The Principal Players

When the service is over he will join the bridegroom's mother as the wedding party proceeds to the vestry for the signing of the register. He also accompanies her out of church then rejoins his wife.

Once the newlyweds have departed, the bride's parents need to be the next to leave the church and be ready to greet the guests at the reception.

The next duty of the bride's father is to make a short speech. Some information on speechmaking appears at the end of this chapter.

Expenditure

When it comes to wedding costs, it might be easier to list the items that the bride's father doesn't pay for. His main expense will probably be the reception and this is often the area where the bridegroom's father offers to share the cost.

The first bill for the bride's father may be for the engagement party. Then he will have the cost of printing invitations and order of service sheets, followed by the bride's dress, wedding cake, flowers for the church and reception, cars and photographer.

He will probably buy a new suit or hire morning dress and his wife will have a new outfit and there will doubtless by other small incidental expenses but they will be as nothing after what has gone before!

TOASTS AND SPEECHES

A subject which brings dread to many and renders others totally dumb is speechmaking. The thought of standing up and 'saying a few words' fills many hearts with something approaching fear. If you feel that 'the speech' is a major obstacle, a copy of *Wedding Speeches & Toasts by Barbara Jeffery* will prove a great help. Apart from guidance on writing and presenting speeches, it contains specimens that you can use or adapt as your own.

Order and Content of Speeches

Toasts and speeches are generally made at the end of the wedding breakfast and it may well fall to the best man to act as toastmaster.

1. The bride's father will be called upon first and the main points of his speech will be:

   a) how proud he and his wife are of their daughter.
   b) a welcome to his new son-in-law with perhaps the old saw about gaining a son not losing a daughter.
   c) also, a welcome to the bridegroom's parents.
   d) words of wisdom and good wishes to the newlyweds.
   e) a toast to the bride and bridegroom.

2. The bridegroom will reply on behalf of his bride and himself along the following lines:

   a) thanking the bride's parents for giving him their daughter in marriage and also for the entire wedding.

b) thanking his own parents for what they have done and thanking the guests for coming and for their gifts.

c) saying how wonderful his bride is, and how fortunate he is.

d) acknowledging the invaluable help given by his best man and proposing a toast to the bridesmaids.

3. The best man replies on behalf of the bridesmaids, expressing:

a) how lucky the groom is to have won such a bride.

b) what a good chap he is anyway and it is what he deserves.

c) the thanks of the bridesmaids for the toast and for their presents.

d) he should also read a selection of telemessages received.

e) he may be asked to tell the guests the programme for the rest of the reception.

The points given are very general ones. It is advisable for speechmakers to find out, early on, what aspects they will be expected to cover in their speeches, and if there are any awkward areas (e.g. family feuds, divorce or separation in the family, etc.) to avoid.

Jokes are acceptable provided that they are not 'blue' or likely to offend any guests. Aim to speak for a maximum of five minutes; you'll be surprised how long five minutes can be when you're standing in front of an audience!

After the three traditional speeches other guests

may wish to say a few words; perhaps the bridegroom's father and sometimes the bride. It is essential that the best man or toastmaster ascertain beforehand whether there are likely to be any other speakers so that he can call upon them before the guests relax, thinking that the speeches have finished.

How to Say It

Once you have a draft of your speech prepared to approximately the right length, keep it with you so you can look at it from time to time, and update it as you gain any new information that you wish to include. Do not try to learn it by heart. Instead, get thoroughly familiar with it, so that you can speak it naturally, glancing at your 'script' from time to time to refresh your memory. You will need to speak a little more slowly and distinctly than normal, but never shout and, if you have a regional accent, don't try to change it.

Rehearsing in front of a mirror, taping your voice as you speak, can be very useful in boosting your self-confidence.

Points to Remember

1• Prepare your speech well beforehand. Use large dark writing or print clearly. It is useful to mark, in colour, pauses and paragraph starts so that you can see these at a glance.

2• Keep it short. Four or five minutes is quite enough.

3• Don't use 'blue' jokes.

4• Try not to repeat yourself or to use the same words or phrases.

5• Make sure you have your speech with you when you arrive at the reception.

6• Don't drink too much before you present your speech.

7• Go to the toilet in good time before making your speech.

8• Speak a little more slowly and clearly than normal, and don't forget to breathe.

9• Don't deviate from your prepared speech. You could end up saying something that you regret.

CHECKLIST 4.1: THE BRIDE

Preparations (*with the bridegroom; **with the bride's mother)

Discuss with minister*: ☐

    Church decorations ☐

    Music ☐

    Organist ☐

    Choir ☐

    Bells ☐

    Order of service ☐

    Fees ☐

    Confetti ☐

    Photographs in church ☐

Choose chief bridesmaid/matron of honour ☐

Choose bridesmaids ☐

Choose pages ☐

Draw up guest list** ☐

Arrange for wedding dress and attachments ☐

    Buy ☐

    Make ☐

    Hire ☐

The Principal Players

Arrange for outfits for bridesmaids and pages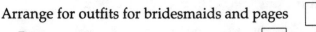

    Buy

    Make

    Hire

Book hairdressing appointment

Order wedding cake and arrange for delivery**

Order bouquets for self and bridesmaids and arrange for delivery**

Order sprays for bride's and groom's mothers, and buttonholes for bridegroom, bride's and groom's fathers, best man and ushers, and arrange for delivery**

Select and book photographer**

Order wedding cars for wedding party to church and to reception**

Write wedding present list

Choose wedding breakfast menu**

Choose wines**

Arrange press announcement

Choose going-away outfit and luggage

Write thank you letters for presents as they arrive

Pack for honeymoon

Wedding Etiquette

On the day

Give gifts to bridesmaids

Take luggage and going-away outfit to
  reception

At the church

Arrive last on father's right arm and proceed
  up the aisle followed by bridesmaids

At chancel steps give bouquet and gloves
  to chief bridesmaid

Allow chief bridesmaid to lift veil

After service, with bridegroom follow minister
  to sign register

Leave church with bridegroom

After photographs, leave first with bridegroom
  for reception

At the reception

Greet guests with bridegroom after parents

With groom, cut cake

After reception, change into going-away outfit

Save flower from bouquet, and toss bouquet on
  leaving

CHECKLIST 4.2: THE BRIDEGROOM

Preparations (*with bride)

Arrange for registrar or clergy*

Choose best man

Choose ushers

Buy wedding ring*

Arrange and pay for wedding outfit

    Buy

    Hire

Plan, book and pay for honeymoon

Organise and pay for stag party

Arrange and pay for car from reception

Buy bridesmaids' gifts

Buy best man's gift

Write speech for reception

Pay for:

    Flowers of bride and attendants

    Buttonholes and sprays

    Car for self and best man to church

    Car for bride and self to reception

Choose going-away outfit and luggage

Pack for honeymoon

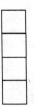

Wedding Etiquette

On the day

Give gift to best man ☐

Give money to best man for church fees ☐

Take luggage and going-away outfit
  to reception ☐

Take going-away car to reception ☐

At the church

Arrive with best man at .... ☐

Step up to altar when bride arrives ☐

After service, with bride follow minister
  to sign register ☐

Leave church with bride ☐

After photographs, leave first with bride for
  reception ☐

At the reception

Greet guests with bride after parents ☐

Respond to toast 'The bride and groom',
  give speech and propose toast to
  'The bridesmaids' ☐

With bride, cut cake ☐

After reception, change into going – away outfit ☐

Collect documents etc. from best man ☐

CHECKLIST 4.3: THE BEST MAN

Preparations

Arrange and pay for own outfit ☐

    Buy ☐

    Hire ☐

Check that groom and ushers have
organised outfits ☐

Write speech for reception ☐

Help to organise stag party ☐

Check parking facilities at church
and reception ☐

Check groom has all necessary documents
for wedding and honeymoon ☐

Arrange for car to take groom and self
to church ☐

On the day

Check that bridegroom's luggage is ready ☐

Check that bridegroom's change of clothes
is ready ☐

Arrange for going-away car to be parked at
reception and keep keys ☐

Have tickets and documents for honeymoon ☐

Have cash for church fees ☐

Wedding Etiquette

Keep wedding rings safe

Have documents for wedding

Collect buttonholes from bride's mother
  and take to church

Collect telemessages and order of service
  sheets from bride's mother

Collect bridegroom at .... o'clock
  and take to church

At the church

Ensure that ushers know duties

Hand order of service sheets to ushers

Make sure bridegroom, groom's father, self and
  ushers have buttonholes, and bride's and
  groom's mothers have sprays

Pay fees to minister

Wait on right of groom and hand over ring at
  appropriate time

After service, with chief bridesmaid follow
  bride and groom to sign register

Leave church with chief bridesmaid

Usher couple to places for photographs

Make sure ushers have arranged transport
  for guests to reception

The Principal Players

After photographs, see couple to car to take them to reception

Leave for reception with bridesmaids after bride and groom

At the reception

Offer drinks to guests

Take charge of any late wedding presents

Place luggage in car for honeymoon

Call on speakers, if there is no toastmaster

Respond to toast of 'The bridesmaids', give speech, read telemessages, give programme for rest of reception

Hand over documents, keys etc. for the honeymoon

See couple to car after reception

After the wedding

Return wedding outfits of groom and self if hired

CHECKLIST 4.4: THE USHERS

Preparations

Arrange and pay for own outfits

    Buy

    Hire

At the church

Arrive at the church at ....

Collect order of service sheets from
best man □

Conduct guests to their pews and hand
out order of service sheets

Ensure guests have transport to reception

At the reception

Offer drinks to guests □

After the wedding

Return outfit if hired □

CHECKLIST 4.5: THE CHIEF BRIDESMAID
(MATRON OF HONOUR)

Preparations

Arrange for own outfit (pay for it unless
 unsuitable for wear at other times)

On the day

Help to dress the bride for the ceremony

Make sure bouquets are ready for bride and
 bridesmaids

Look after bridesmaids and pages

At the church

Assemble with bridesmaids and pages in
 church porch

Arrange bride's dress, veil and train for
 procession up the aisle

Take bride's bouquet and gloves at
 chancel steps

Lift bride's veil

After service, with best man follow bride and
 groom to sign register

Return bouquet and gloves to bride in vestry

Leave church with best man after
 bride and groom

Wedding Etiquette

After photographs, leave for reception
with best man and other bridesmaids,
after bride and groom

At the reception

Offer drinks to guests

Check that bride's going-away outfit is ready

Check that bride's luggage is ready

Help bride change into going – away clothes

See bride to car

After the wedding

Return bride's and own outfit if hired

CHECKLIST 4.6: THE BRIDE'S MOTHER

Preparations (**with bride)

Draw up guest list**

Arrange printing of invitations

Arrange printing of order of service cards

Send invitations

List acceptances received

Draw up final guest list

Prepare seating plan

Arrange wedding outfit

    Buy

    Make

Order bouquets for bride and bridesmaids
and arrange for delivery**

Order sprays for self and groom's mother,
and buttonholes for bridegroom, bride's
and groom's fathers, best man and ushers,
and arrange for delivery**

Arrange church decorations

Select and book photographer**

Make arrangements for reception at. . . . .

    Home

    Hotel

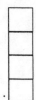

Wedding Etiquette

Restaurant □

Private Hall □

Make catering arrangements □

Self □

Professional caterers □

Choose wedding breakfast menu** □

Choose wines** □

Arrange for table decorations □

Arrange accommodation for guests □

Arrange for printed napkins □

Arrange for printed place setting cards □

Arrange for musicians/entertainment □

Order wedding cars for wedding party
to church and to reception □

Order wedding cake and arrange
for delivery** □

Buy wedding cake boxes □

Arrange for neighbour to lock house after
bride and father have left □

At the church

Arrive before the bride at .... □

After service, with groom's father follow bride's
father and groom's mother to sign register □

The Principal Players

Leave church with groom's father

After photographs, leave for reception with husband after bridesmaids

At the reception

With bride's father, greet guests

When all guests have arrived, give signal for wedding breakfast to begin

Arrange display of gifts

Arrange changing room for bride

Arrange display of proof photographs

Take photograph orders from family and guests

After the wedding

Send pieces of cake to relatives/friends who could not attend wedding

Give order to photographer

Collect and distribute photographs

CHECKLIST 4.7: THE BRIDE'S FATHER

Preparations

Arrange for wedding outfit ☐

    Buy ☐

    Hire ☐

Write speech for reception ☐

Pay for:

    Reception ☐

    Flowers to decorate church and reception ☐

    Wedding dress ☐

    Wedding cake ☐

    Photographer ☐

    Wedding cars ☐

    Press announcement ☐

    Hairdressing ☐

    Invitations and order of service printing ☐

Keep buttonhole at home when other sprays/ buttonholes taken to church ☐

At the church

Arrive last with bride on right arm and proceed up aisle ☐

The Principal Players

At appropriate moment, give bride's right
hand to minister

After service, with groom's mother follow best
man and chief bridesmaid to sign register

Leave church with groom's mother

After photographs, leave for reception with
wife after bridesmaids

At the reception

With bride's mother greet guests

When called by best man, give speech and
propose toast to bride and groom

5

THE MARRIAGE CEREMONY

Before the ceremony itself takes place, there will almost certainly be an opportunity to attend a rehearsal in the church. The minister will run through all the details of the service and explain the roles of each of the principal members of the wedding party.

It is best if the whole wedding party can attend the rehearsal, but if that is not possible it will help if the best man can be present so that he can later advise anyone who is unsure of the correct procedures.

CHURCH OF ENGLAND WEDDINGS

If you are getting married in an Anglican church, you should have already discussed with the minister whether the service is to be traditional or if it is to be conducted according to an Alternative Service Book version. The minister may have his own very definite opinions about this, but in fact both ceremonies are very moving.

If the parents of either the bride or the bridegroom are divorced, a little tact and cooperation all round will help to ensure that the wedding is still a happy occasion – both for them, and for the couple about to be married.

At the church, the seating arrangements are slightly altered. If the bride's parents are divorced, then her mother will be shown to the first pew on the left – hand side of the church. She may be with her new husband, or, if she has not remarried, with a close relative. The bride's father takes his seat in the second or third pew, also with his new partner if he has remarried. The same arrangements apply to the bridegroom's parents if they are divorced.

Twenty minutes or so before a Church of England wedding is due to begin, the guests will start to arrive. The bride's family and friends are conducted to the left-hand seats of the church and the bridegroom's family and friends to those on the right-hand. The bridegroom and the best man are seated in the front pews. The bride's mother usually travels to the church with the bridesmaids, who remain in the church porch until the bride and her father arrive.

When the bride has taken her place at the church entrance, the organist will play the entrance music. At this point the congregation rises. The bride takes her father's right arm and they walk down the aisle followed by the bridesmaids. If it is a full choral service the minister may meet the bride in the porch and the procession will be led by the choir, followed by the minister, the bride and her father and the bridesmaids.

The bridegroom and the best man meet the party at the chancel steps. The bride stands on the left of the bridegroom, and her father to her left, but slightly to the rear. The best man positions himself on the right of the bridegroom and, like the father, slightly to the rear. (After the bride's father has given away his daughter, he can take his seat next to his wife in the front pew. The best man can also step to one side after he has presented the ring.)

At this point the chief bridesmaid steps forward to take the bride's bouquet or, if there are no bridesmaids, it may be handed to her father, who in turn may give it to his wife. The bouquet should be returned to the bride before she leaves the church – usually at the signing of the register.

The ceremony then begins. The minister first explains the significance of marriage according to the Scriptures. He then calls on the congregation – and the bride and bridegroom – to declare if there is any reason why the couple may not lawfully marry.

The minister then asks each of the couple in turn whether they promise to love, comfort, honour and forsaking all others (in the modern version) protect the other ... 'as long as you both shall live' to which they reply 'I will'.

The bridegroom takes the bride's right hand in his, and they exchange vows 'to have and to hold, from this day forward; for better, for worse, for richer, for poorer, in sickness and in health, to love and to cherish till death us do part'.

The best man gives the ring to the minister, and the bridegroom places it on the third finger of the bride's left hand – or sometimes rings are exchanged. The bridegroom then makes his promise to the bride, in the modern version as follows:

'I give you this ring
as a sign of our marriage.
With my body I honour you,
all that I am I give to you,
and all that I have I share with you,
within the love of God,
Father, Son and Holy Spirit.'

The bride responds with the same promise, beginning 'I receive this ring ...' and the minister then pronounces them man and wife. After the marriage, and before signing the register, the minister will sometimes give a short address, especially if one or both of the married couple are known to him.

When the service is concluded, the wedding party move into the vestry to sign the register. The best man and the chief bridesmaid usually act as the two witnesses. Everyone has a chance to relax now, and one or two photographs are usually taken at the signing.

Coming out of the church, the bride takes the left arm of the bridegroom and they are followed by any small bridesmaids; the chief bridesmaid and the best man; the bride's mother and the bridegroom's father; the bridegroom's mother and the bride's father; and the bridesmaids, often escorted by the ushers. Relatives leave next and are followed by special guests and then friends.

Outside, there will be a good deal of milling around as the wedding photographs are taken. Confetti (if it is permitted) will most likely be thrown when the bride and bridegroom decide it is time to leave for the reception.

PLACES DURING THE
CHURCH OF ENGLAND CEREMONY

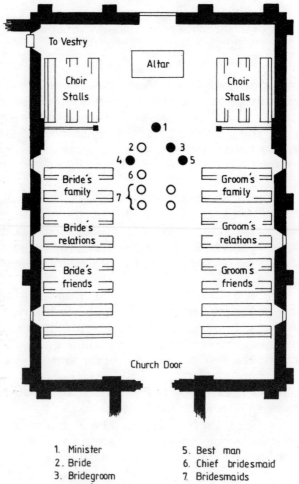

1. Minister
2. Bride
3. Bridegroom
4. Bride's father
5. Best man
6. Chief bridesmaid
7. Bridesmaids

THE PROCESSION TO THE VESTRY AFTER THE CHURCH OF ENGLAND CEREMONY

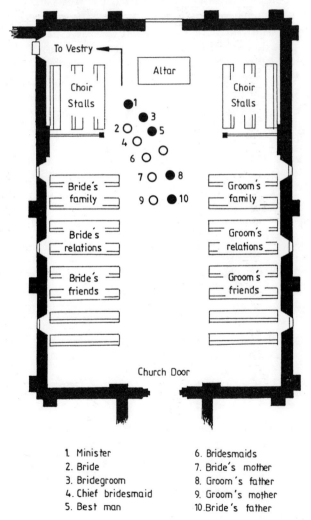

1. Minister
2. Bride
3. Bridegroom
4. Chief bridesmaid
5. Best man
6. Bridesmaids
7. Bride's mother
8. Groom's father
9. Groom's mother
10. Bride's father

REGISTER OFFICE WEDDINGS

The reasons that couples opt for a register office wedding are various, not least of them of course being financial. The cost of a full-scale church wedding is now said to average more than £6,000. No matter how that sort of cost is shared, many couples obviously feel that there is a strong case in favour of a register office wedding.

Because there are generally size limitations in a register office there will be room for only a few guests to accompany the couple and their two witnesses. Everybody should arrive about ten minutes before the ceremony to ensure that it starts on time, as there will probably be another wedding following shortly. The tradition of the bride arriving with her father is not always followed; sometimes the prospective bride and groom arrive together.

The ceremony takes about ten to fifteen minutes and will be conducted by the Superintendent Registrar. The couple must state they know of no legal impediment to marrying and will be reminded of the solemn and binding nature of the vows which they will repeat after the registrar. The ring or rings are exchanged and the relevant documents signed by the couple and the witnesses.

FREE CHURCH WEDDINGS

Most of the Free Church buildings have been registered by a Superintendent of Marriages as buildings in which marriages may be solemnised. Ministers of these churches, be they United Reform, Baptist, Methodist or other Protestant church, are generally registered as 'authorised' persons to conduct the marriage service and also to act as the registrar, which simply means keeping the marriage register. If such authorisation has not been obtained a Superintendent Registrar, or his deputy, must be present to record the wedding although the minister may still conduct the ceremony. Alternatively, a civil ceremony may be conducted by the Superintendent Registrar in his office.

The order of service is very similar to that used in the Church of England, with variations amongst the different denominations. After the bridal procession arrives in front of the minister, together with the bridegroom and best man, the service begins with a declaration of intent. The bride and groom in turn will say:

'I do solemnly declare that I know not of any lawful impediment why I ..... may not be joined in matrimony to .....'

After the minister has asked the congregation if they know of any lawful objection to the marriage, the couple exchange vows and proceed with the ceremony of the ring followed by the blessing. After the service the newlyweds and two witnesses sign the register.

On the question of the re-marriage of divorced persons it is very much a matter of each minister considering each case on its own merits. He may have very strong views on the subject or he may be willing to give careful consideration to the matter and agree to conduct a church service.

ROMAN CATHOLIC WEDDINGS

As with all marriages outside the Church of England, the couple must give notice of their intention to marry to the local Superintendent Registrar (or registrars if they live in different districts). Often the priest or one of his parishioners will be authorised to register the marriage, in which case the registrar is not required to be present at the wedding.

The marriage ceremony may be conducted during Mass (called a Nuptial Mass) or outside Mass – usually when one of the couple is not a Roman Catholic. However, the rite of marriage is the same in either case.

The priest first addresses the bride and bridegroom on the significance of marriage within the Church: it is regarded as a sacrament which will 'enrich and strengthen' them so that the union will be one of 'mutual and lasting fidelity'.

The couple have to declare no lawful impediment to marriage; they promise to be faithful to each other and to accept they bring up children within the Roman Catholic faith. The priest invites them to declare their consent to marry 'according to the rite of our holy Mother the Church' to which each replies 'I will'.

Right hands joined, the couple then call upon the congregation to witness the marriage, and make their vows, 'to have and to hold from this day forward ... till death do us part'.

The priest confirms them in marriage and the rings are blessed and exchanged – or only one may be given – using the following words:

> 'I (Christian name only) take this ring as a
> sign of my love and fidelity. In the name
> of the Father and of the Son and of the
> Holy Spirit.'

JEWISH WEDDINGS

When Jewish people marry, they are required to give notice to the registrar, but the marriage may be solemnised in a synagogue or private house. When a synagogue or house is used, the secretary of the synagogue to which the man belongs must take down the necessary particulars.

The ceremony, when held in a synagogue, varies in the form it takes. The bride and bridegroom stand under a canopy – a *chuppah* – which is a reminder of the time when the Israelites were forced to live in tents. The couple's parents join in the ceremony by standing under the canopy with them and supporting them. Behind are their relations and friends. The best man stands behind and to the left of the bridegroom.

The rabbi delivers a short address to the couple. Then the bridegroom turns to the bride who stands to his right and before placing the ring on her finger he says: 'Behold, thou art consecrated unto me by this ring, according to the law of Moses and of Israel.' The bride should wear no other rings or jewellery, not even her engagement ring.

The next step is the reading and signing of the Hebrew marriage contract. The man promises to be a true and faithful husband, and to protect, support, love, honour and cherish his bride. She promises to be true and faithful and to love, honour and cherish him.

Following the vows, the Seven Benedictions are recited and the couple drink wine, twice from the same vessel; then the bridegroom dashes the glass to the ground. Drinking the wine reminds the couple that they are required to share each other's pleasures and halve each other's troubles. The broken glass symbolises the weakness of marriage without love.

Before the ceremony is concluded, the following covenant is signed:

On the ... day of the week, the ... day of the month of ... in the year ... corresponding to the ... of ... the Holy covenant of marriage was entered into, in ..., between the bridegroom ..., and his bride, ...

The said bridegroom made the following declaration to his bride: 'Be thou my wife according to the Law of Moses and of Israel. I faithfully promise that I will be a true husband unto thee. I will honour and cherish thee; I will work for thee; I will protect and support thee; and will provide all that is necessary for thy due sustenance, even as it beseemeth a Jewish husband to do. I also take upon myself all such further obligations for thy maintenance during thy lifetime as are prescribed by our religious statutes'.

And the said bride plighted her troth unto him, in affection and with sincerity, and has thus taken upon herself the fulfilment of all the duties incumbent upon a Jewish wife.

This covenant of marriage was duly executed and witnessed this day according to the usage of Israel.

QUAKER WEDDINGS

When a wedding is to take place according to the usages of the Society of Friends, the arrangements come under the care of the Society's registering officer for the area concerned.

It should be noted that besides giving notice to the registering officer, notice must also be given to the local Superintendent Registrar in the usual way. The Society's registering officer will ensure that the Quaker regulations are followed and that, if they are satisfactorily completed, the meeting for worship to solemnise the marriage is duly approved.

At the ceremony, the usual custom is for the bride and bridegroom to sit surrounded by their relations and friends, and then for the two to stand at a moment when they feel it is right. Holding hands, the man makes the following declaration:

'Friends, I take this my friend, ..., to be my wife, promising through divine assistance, to be unto her a loving and faithful husband so long as we both on earth shall live.'

The bride makes a similar declaration. A certificate is then signed by the couple and two witnesses, stating that the couple made the necessary declarations, that they fulfilled the legal obligations and were duly married. All those present are invited to sign the certificate after the meeting is over.

No ring need appear at the ceremony, but sometimes one ring is given or rings may be exchanged after the declaration.

WEDDINGS ABROAD

A fairly recent innovation for people looking for something novel in the way of marriage is to travel abroad to get wed. There are travel companies who will arrange the whole package deal for you. The favourite destinations are some of the islands of the West Indies, the Seychelles and Mauritius. It could be seen as travelling to your honeymoon destination first, then getting married.

Some couples may take members of their family, or friends with them, but if they arrive alone the travel companies may arrange for a best man and bridesmaids in addition to all the legal arrangements, hotel and travel, not forgetting all the 'extras', such as flowers, wedding cake, reception and video of the ceremony.

If the idea of marrying abroad appeals to you, but you would prefer to make the arrangements yourself, you should be especially careful. The problems you might encounter are numerous and will involve you in a great deal of correspondence with the various authorities.

6

THE RECEPTION

After the wedding ceremony comes the reception and in the case of the traditional English wedding this follows a certain pattern. It may be a very large reception with hundreds of guests or a small, informal gathering, but in either case there is a very similar pattern to the proceedings.

The first decision regarding the reception, which needs to be made some months in advance of the wedding, is where the reception should be held: hall, hotel or house. With a large number of guests, the choice is between hall and hotel, and in either case an early booking will be necessary. An average size house can probably accommodate only thirty or forty guests, but there is an attractive alternative, if the house in question has a large garden. It is possible to hire marquees which can be set up a few days beforehand and which contain all the necessary fitments such as lights and suitable wooden or mat flooring.

A decision about the catering arrangements will probably be made at the same time as the choice of venue is decided. Naturally a reception held in a hotel will mean that the hotel will arrange everything at an inclusive charge per guest. They will also provide rooms in which the bride and groom will be able to change their clothes during the reception.

Unless some members of the family are particularly adept in the catering line, it is probably a wise choice to call in specialist caterers, whether the reception is in a hall or a private house. It might seem feasible to lay on a tasty spread for thirty or so guests in a small, informal gathering at home, but with a hundred and one other things to think of on the big day, the professional touch can often be worth that extra cost. A booking in a local hall no doubt provides the most options: outside caterers or do it yourself, sit-down meal or buffet. What the hall might not have is a suitable room in which the bride and groom can change into their going-away outfits, so a suitable arrangement will need to be made.

A Formal Reception

A formal or semi-formal reception, will have a receiving line to welcome the guests. This usually consists of the bride's mother and father, the bridegroom's mother and father and the bride and bridegroom themselves – in that order. This applies whether or not either set of parents is divorced. New partners are not normally included in the receiving line. If a large number of guests has been invited and you want to speed proceedings up, the bride and bridegroom can do the receiving on their own.

The Reception

On entering, the guests are usually presented with a glass of wine or an aperitif, and when the last guest has been received everyone looks for their name card and takes their place at the tables. Sometimes seating arrangements are left to the guests to make their own choices. If there are separate bar and dining areas, early arrivals can wait comfortably in the bar until everyone is assembled.

Seating arrangements vary according to the number of guests and the layout of the tables. For a formal reception, however, there will be a 'top table' for the principal members of the wedding party and the attendants (see diagram on page 114). Since it is an honour to sit at the top table, be careful not to hurt anyone's feelings by including a guest who is not also a member of the wedding party. An aunt who has flown in from Australia for the wedding may, however, be classed as an exception!

The bride and the two mothers usually work out how best to seat the other guests. If there are complications due to a parental divorce, seating arrangements at the top table should be discussed with all the parties concerned. Depending on how co-operative they are likely to be, there should be no problem in finding everyone a place. You will probably want to aim at some interchanging between the families – but not so much that noone knows what to say to each other.

If the bride's parents are divorced and she has been brought up by her mother and a stepfather, he may be asked to make the first speech and propose the main toast. However, the exact arrangements will vary according to the individual circumstances and should be discussed and agreed beforehand.

The most important thing is that personal feelings about ex-partners do not get out of hand and interfere with the success of the wedding – and if the situation is handled with dignity and understanding, there is no reason why they should.

After the last course is completed (or alternatively, about halfway through proceedings) the cakecutting ceremony and the toasts and speeches take place.

The first to speak is the bride's father who stands and says a few words before proposing the main toast: 'Health and happiness to the bride and bridegroom.' The bridegroom responds briefly, thanking the bride's parents and the guests, and ends by proposing a toast to the health of the bridesmaids. The best man follows by replying for the bridesmaids and reading out the congratulatory telemessages. The bride may also elect to say a few words.

All the speeches should be kept short and informal. If they can be witty without being offensive, so much the better. However, a sincere approach often goes down just as well, so if you have any doubts about your abilities as a humorist, it is best not to try.

The cake should have been ordered some weeks before and delivered to the reception on the day of the wedding. Icing on a traditional wedding cake can be very thick so it will help if this is already cut through. The bride holds the knife in her right hand, with the bridegroom's right hand on hers, and her left hand on top. After the first slice has been successfully dealt with, the cake can be taken away and cut into smaller pieces for the guests to eat with their coffee. You may wish to rescue the top tier to keep for a christening. Use cake boxes to send pieces of the cake to people who could not attend the wedding.

If there is to be dancing, the bride and bridegroom will be first on to the floor, followed by the chief bridesmaid and the best man, and members of the two families.

After a while spent chatting to the guests, the couple slip away to change into going-away clothes, returning for a few minutes to say their final good-byes before going on honeymoon. Traditionally, just before they leave, the bride tosses her bouquet to a bridesmaid or a female guest who, tradition has it, will be the next in line for marriage.

CHECKLIST 6.1: SEATING PLACES AT THE RECEPTION

Arrange seating plan

Top Table

1. Groom's mother
2. Bride's father
3. Bride
4. Bridegroom
5. Bride's mother

6. Groom's father
7. Chief bridesmaid
8. Best man
9. Groom's family
10. Bride's family

Variations on the seating may be made although the top table is usually reserved for the wedding party. Alternating the sexes is usual. The families can be mixed.

CHECKLIST 6.2: AT THE RECEPTION

As the guests arrive they should be greeted by:

The bride's father and mother ☐

The groom's father and mother ☐

The bride and groom ☐

Attendants and ushers should offer drinks
and chat pleasantly ☐

When all the guests have arrived, the hostess
(the bride's mother) should give the signal
for the wedding breakfast to begin ☐

If champagne is used for toasts only, it
should be left until after the meal and
served just before the speeches begin ☐

After the meal, the best man calls upon
the bride's father to speak ☐

The bride's father gives a speech and proposes
the toast to 'The bride and groom' ☐

The bridegroom responds, gives a speech and
proposes a toast to 'The bridesmaids' ☐

The best man responds on behalf of the
bridesmaids, gives a speech and reads
out a selection of telemessages ☐

The bride and groom cut the cake ☐

The bride and groom lead the dancing, followed
by the best man and the chief bridesmaid,
and the parents of the bride and groom ☐

7

THE HONEYMOON

If the wedding ceremony and reception need careful thought and planning, so does the first trip that the bride and bridegroom will take together as a married couple. Most people will want to have a honeymoon, and the tradition of starting on the honeymoon immediately after the wedding is still followed by the majority of couples who get married today.

Apart from the question of cost, the most important factor is to take a honeymoon which will appeal to both of you. A honeymoon in which the interests of one partner are followed while the other trails along with little enthusiasm is hardly the best way to start married life. So there should be a discussion well before the wedding: read through the brochures together, and book the holiday well in advance.

When you're thinking about where to go for the honeymoon, remember to take into account the date of the wedding. If you're getting married in the winter months, and you want sun, you will have to pay for it. Alternatively, you could opt for a honeymoon in a city, such as London or Paris, where the attractions are not so dependent on the weather.

Don't be shy about admitting your new status: some travel firms offer honeymoon trips complete with free champagne and four-poster beds, and hotels will often make a special effort to see that the honeymoon stay is as enjoyable as possible.

Honeymoons abroad also mean you have to check on passports, travel tickets, travellers cheques, hotel reservations, foreign currency and medical insurance, as well as any inoculations that may be required. Don't leave it all to the last minute. You will have enough to do in the run up to the wedding without worrying about the possible after effects of an injection against cholera!

Finally, don't be too surprised if the honeymoon doesn't live up to all your expectations. The first few weeks of marriage are rarely without their problems. Two adults who have already developed personalities and ways of their own have to learn to adjust to one another. Relax, take things as they come, and you will soon find yourself looking back with affection on what will almost certainly be one of the most memorable holidays of your life.

8

WEDDING SUPERSTITIONS

Most of us like to play the superstition game at one time or another and weddings in particular come in for a whole range of sayings and warnings – which are fun if you take them with 'a pinch of salt'!

When it comes to deciding on the date it is unlucky to marry on your birthday; however it is particularly lucky if husband and wife share the same birthday, although they must be a year or two apart.

There are many sayings intended for the bride. The need for her to wear 'something old, something new, something borrowed and something blue' at the wedding is well known. It is generally considered unlucky for the bride to make her own dress – even professional dressmakers rarely do – and it is even more unlucky to try on the full bridal array too soon, especially if she sees herself in a full length mirror. She can, of course, leave off a glove or a shoe out of respect for the old tradition!

Did you know that an old veil is thought to be luckier than a new one? This is particularly true if borrowed from a woman who is happily married, or if it is an heirloom of the bride's family. The good fortune and/or fertility of the earlier marriages passes with the veil to its new wearer.

The colour of the bride's dress is supposed to be a faithful portent of the future:

> White is a symbol of purity and of high virtues.
> Green typifies youth, hope and happiness.
> Red is a sign of vigour, courage and great passion.
> (There may be a touch of jealousy in its reading, however.)
> Violet denotes dignity, pride and a condition of high ideals.

The wedding procession is not overlooked. The bride must leave her home by the front door with her right foot foremost. It is considered lucky if the sun shines or she sees a rainbow on the way or meets a black cat or a chimney sweep 'in his blacks'.

The modern custom of sending a piece of wedding cake to friends and relatives not present has its roots in a desire for them to share its luck-bringing properties and one old saying advises the bride to keep a piece of the cake – if she does her husband will be faithful to her.

The following dates are reckoned to be especially lucky for weddings:

January	2	4	11	19	21
February	1	3	10	19	21
March	3	5	12	20	23
April	2	4	12	20	22

Wedding Etiquette

May	2	4	12	20	23	
June	1	3	11	19	21	
July	1	3	12	19	21	31
August	2	11	18	20		31
September	1	9	16	18	28	
October			15	18	27	29
November	5	11	13	22	25	
December	1	8	10	19	23	29

Other superstitions about the wedding day are of a more general nature.

• 'Happy the bride whom the sun shines on' may be a well-known saying. But did you know that one way to guard against rain is to feed your cat on the morning of the wedding? (If you're getting married in Germany – steer clear of cats. Each drop of rain is looked upon as a blessing on the marriage.)

• It is a good sign if the bride is awakened on the day by the song of a bird – and also if she discovers a spider in the folds of her dress!

• It's bad luck to break anything – especially a mirror - on the wedding morning, or to lose the heel of a shoe.

• With each glance in the mirror, the bride is supposed to add something to her make-up or clothing, even if it's only a pair of gloves.

• It's bad luck for the couple to meet in the morning before the wedding – but good luck if they smile at each other when they meet in the church.

- A bride is not supposed to weep before the marriage, but she may do so as much as she likes afterwards: this proves that she is not a witch, who could shed only three tears from her left eye.

- If the bride sees a lamb, a dove, a spider, a toad, or a black cat on her way to the church, it is a sign of good luck; but it is reckoned as a very bad omen if she should encounter a funeral party, or if a pig crosses the road in front of the wedding car.

The Bridegroom

Rather fewer superstitions surround the conduct of the bridegroom on his wedding day. All will be well so long as he does not see his bride in her wedding dress before he meets her in the church and does not drop the ring before putting it on the bride's finger. If she has to assist him in this, he may expect to be ruled by her in the future. It is also considered unlucky to buy the engagement and wedding rings on the same day. He should pay the church fees (through the best man) with an odd sum of money, carry a small mascot in his pocket and on no account turn back for anything after leaving for the church.

After the honeymoon, the husband should carry his wife over the threshold of their new home. When this is done, both will be rewarded with all the good fortune they could wish for.

The Bridesmaids

Finally, for the bridesmaids, there is one unfortunate saying: 'Three times a bridesmaid, never a bride'.

9

WEDDING ANNIVERSARIES

Most people like to celebrate wedding anniversaries with presents and perhaps have an evening out at a favourite restaurant or theatre.

Traditionally, certain materials are associated with individual years in the marriage series, the idea being that anniversary presents in those years should be made out of the particular materials named. So, if you want to uphold the custom – flowers and boxes of chocolates notwithstanding – the list below gives the names generally associated with each year. They do vary slightly, however; paper is sometimes given for the first year, leather for the twelfth, ivory for the thirteenth, wool for the fortieth, and silk for the forty-fifth.

Anniversary	*Wedding*
First	Cotton
Second	Paper
Third	Leather
Fourth	Books
Fifth	Wood

Wedding Etiquette

Anniversary	*Wedding*
Sixth	Sugar
Seventh	Wool
Eighth	Bronze
Ninth	Pottery
Tenth	Tin
Twelfth	Silk and Fine Linen
Thirteenth	Lace
Fourteenth	Ivory
Fifteenth	Crystal
Twentieth	China
Twenty-fifth	Silver
Thirtieth	Pearl
Thirty-fifth	Coral
Fortieth	Ruby
Forty-fifth	Sapphire
Fiftieth	Gold
Fifty-fifth	Emerald
Sixtieth	Diamond
Seventieth	Platinum
Seventy-fifth	Diamond

Notes

Notes

Notes